THERE'S A LAKE IN MY BACKYARD!

By Seth Lynch

Gareth Stevens
PUBLISHING

Please visit our website, www.garethstevens.com. For a free color catalog of all our high-quality books, call toll free 1-800-542-2595 or fax 1-877-542-2596.

Cataloging-in-Publication Data

Names: Lynch, Seth.
Title: There's a lake in my backyard! / Seth Lynch.
Description: New York: Gareth Stevens, 2017. | Series: Backyard biomes | Includes index.
Identifiers: ISBN 9781482455632 (pbk.) | ISBN 9781482455656 (library bound) | ISBN 9781482455649 (6 pack)
Subjects: LCSH: Lakes–Juvenile literature.| Lake ecology–Juvenile literature.
Classification: LCC GB1603.8 L96 2017 | DDC 577.63–dc23

Published in 2017 by
Gareth Stevens Publishing
111 East 14th Street, Suite 349
New York, NY 10003

Designer: Andrea Davison-Bartolotta and Bethany Perl
Editor: Kristen Nelson

Photo credits: p. 1 Irina Mos/Shutterstock.com; pp. 2–24 (background texture) wongwean/Shutterstock.com; p. 5 bikeriderlondon/Shutterstock.com; p. 7 Galyna Andrushko/Shutterstock.com; p. 9 (main photo) Evgeny Sayfutdinov/Shutterstock.com; p. 9 (map) Ridvan EFE/Shutterstock.com; p. 11 EvgenySHCH/Shutterstock.com; p. 13 Auhustsinovich/Shutterstock.com; p. 15 Nicola Bertolini/Shutterstock.com; p. 17 (plankton) MaryValery/Shutterstock.com; p. 17 (girl) Olga1818/Shutterstock.com; p. 17 (eagle) Tomacco/Shutterstock.com; p. 17 (arrows) schab/Shutterstock.com; p. 17 (background) Dzm1try/Shutterstock.com; p. 17 (fish) Graphicworld/Shutterstock.com; p. 19 (Lake Superior) John McCormick/Shutterstock.com; p. 19 (map) IndianSummer/Shutterstock.com; p. 21 itakdalee/Shutterstock.com.

Printed in the United States of America

CPSIA compliance information: Batch #CW17GS: For further information contact Gareth Stevens, New York, New York at 1-800-542-2595.

CONTENTS

Boldface words appear in the glossary.

Fun and Important

Lakes are fun places to swim and take boat rides. You might even have one in your backyard! They're an important **biome**, too. Many plants grow in and around lakes. Lakes **provide** food and water to both people and animals.

Lake Features

A lake is a large body of water **surrounded** by land. The land around a lake can be rocky, sandy, or muddy, depending on where the lake is. Some lakes have forests around them. Others have roads or homes built next to them.

7

Most lakes hold **freshwater**. Lakes can be miles across and thousands of feet deep. The deepest lake on Earth is Lake Baikal in central Asia. Its deepest point is 5,370 feet (1,637 m) deep!

Lake Baikal

Asia

Wildlife

Many different kinds of animals live in and around lakes.

Fish, such as bass and trout, are found in some lakes. Snakes are common, too. Birds, such as ducks, go to lakes to make nests and find food.

11

Plants have **adapted** to life in lakes. Some have strong roots to stay in place as the water moves. Others have **flexible** stems that let them move with the water. Duckweed floats on top of the water!

duckweed

13

Plankton is an important group of **organisms** living in lakes. It includes tiny plants and animals that are food for bugs and other animals. It also includes some algae, which are plantlike organisms that grow in lakes.

algae

15

A Food Chain

The lake biome in your backyard is home to a **food chain**! Plankton is food for bugs or small fish. Then, bigger fish eat the small fish or bugs. Finally, birds, **mammals**, and even people eat the bigger fish.

eagle

big fish

small fish

plankton

Great Lakes

Lake Superior, Lake Huron, and Lake Michigan are some of Earth's biggest lakes. They're part of the five Great Lakes, which are on the border between the United States and Canada. Each of the Great Lakes has its own biome.

Lake Superior

19

Take Care of Your Lake

Trash and other **pollution** harm lakes. People sometimes use too much water from lakes, too. A lake isn't just part of your backyard—it's home to many plants and animals. Keep it clean, and don't waste it!

GLOSSARY

adapt: to change to suit conditions

biome: a natural community of plants and animals, such as a forest or desert

flexible: able to bend easily

food chain: the way in which animals and plants pass energy within a community

freshwater: water that is not salty

mammal: a warm-blooded animal that has a backbone and hair, breathes air, and feeds milk to its young

organism: a living thing

pollution: matter that can harm an area

provide: to supply what is needed

surround: to circle completely

FOR MORE INFORMATION

BOOKS

Kopp, Megan. *Rivers and Lakes Inside Out*. New York, NY: Crabtree Publishing, 2015.

Silverman, Buffy. *Let's Visit the Lake*. Minneapolis, MN: Lerner Publications, 2017.

WEBSITES

Freshwater
kids.nceas.ucsb.edu/biomes/freshwater.html
Read about the plants and animals that live in freshwater biomes.

Great Lakes Water Life Photo Gallery
www.glerl.noaa.gov/seagrant/GLWL/Fish/Fish.html
What fish live in the Great Lakes? Find out here!

INDEX